W9-CKT-436

everyone knows

that dragons don't exist

Ahsahta Press
Boise, Idaho

The New Series
#58

Dragon Logic

Stephanie Strickland

AHSAHTA PRESS

Boise State University
Boise, Idaho 83725-1525
ahsahtapress.org

Cover design by Quemadura
Book design by Janet Holmes
Printed in Canada

LIBRARY OF CONGRESS CATALOGING-IN-PUBLICATION DATA

Strickland, Stephanie.
[Poems. Selections]
Dragon logic / Stephanie Strickland.
pages ; cm.—(The new series ; #58)
ISBN 978-1-934103-45-6 (pbk. : alk. paper)
ISBN 1-934103-45-4 (pbk. : alk. paper)
I. Title.
PS3569.T69543D73 2013
2013011005

ACKNOWLEDGMENTS

Grateful acknowledgment is made to the following publications—and to their editors—in which these poems (in this form or another, often as numbered sections of the Huracan's Harp sequence) first appeared:

1913 a journal of forms; Barrow Street; Bird Dog; Boston Review (online); *Colorado Review; Court Green; Critiphoria* (online); *Dandelion Magazine* (Canada); *Denver Quarterly; Electronic Poetry Review* (online); *Fence; Gulf Coast; jubilat; Mad Hatters' Review* (online); *MiPOesias* (online); *New American Writing; Notre Dame Review; Octopus* (online); *P-Queue; Saint Elizabeth Street* (online); *Vlak, Volt; Women's Studies Quarterly, Technology Issue.*

A Sing Economy, Flim Forum Anthology 2 published "RUPTURE is complete with the CD," "GREAT Pan is dead," "INVOKING Tzimtzum Persephone contracted Peirce," as "SUBLIME zimzum Persephone contracted Peirce pure zero," "SUBJECT: [webartery] Short Graphism," and "THE SAME interaction the same charge and enormous."

The &NOW Awards: The Best Innovative Writing, 2009 re-published "TECHNICIANS in blue collarless jumpsuits trained," *Fence*; "MINIMUM" as "*MINIMUM* somethings consist altogether of," *P-Queue*; "opening hands of clock time ∨ ← see," *P-Queue*; and "ALGORITHM" as "ALGORITHM RECIPE," *Women's Studies Quarterly, Technology Issue.*

Zoland Poetry 5 published "BURNING BRIAR SCANNING TUNNEL" as "burning briar scanning tunnel," "UNSOLVED PROBLEMS" as "unsolved problems," and "YOU already know what to do" as "already."

"VARIETIES of ecocide : does it matter," "INDIGO maroon purple Tyrant," and "IN-DIVISIBLE plays X-streame dial with her cousin" as "IN-DIVISIBLE plays X-tream dial with her cousin" first appeared in *Chicago Review.*

Contents

Dragon Maps

°Codemakers

Afterword

. . . there are songs to sing beyond / the human

—PAUL CELAN°

Breathturn

Why do the poets of the present not speak of it?

—RICHARD P. FEYNMAN°

Lectures on Physics

e-Dragons

THE RADIO hope
     access to the dead
     access to the lightfuzz that lived
          in crystal sets slipping feet tripping
          wings in vacuum tube towers
          in the Hendrix° amplifier
          from the back
          cities of snubnose glass open to view
in old radios was the RCA°
     dog fooled
     as fully as I was *people*
in the radio all I meant
by people in the radio too delicate too breakable
          for my harsh moves
          too wrapped in an upswept case
               with a dial face
               intermittent as clouds
               static
               music
          too apt to erupt or be unplugged
          too innerly unreachable
          by my clumsy moth

FIREFLIES arriving moon green
        flashers on the Abacus of Al-Farabi°

electrochromic mirrors' dissolving
        messages

pour through a hole in the earlid eyelap lingual
        lobe

sound fills urban
        space as vascular body

streamed transmission signal speech waste sails
        to the stars moves out beyond detection

Silence : Fire towering in sand
        Burning Man

rain forest replaced
        suddenly exchanged with

sparkle mist phosphor'd
        shadows

A ZEPHYR streaming bareback knife-sharp spins
pinging aerial in air scanning rapt in candescent blazing
paths of no return

rides

weight pounds of gray
skin wrinkled to the ground
to the stool where
lifted foot

cranium chambered cairn and passage grave
bulging Neolithic earth mound enclosing the vault

calibrated stone to this standard surpasses us
lost too inner touch on bone pale solstice beam

dervish Snow Queen covens of raven rim her platinum
cloak downed traces of her sledge paused print a fine grid

on the peregrine's° pouring away world of no attachment
tilting wakes twisting falls sinking panes of land and water

dive-bomb raptor-force 2 0 0 miles per hour stoop!
copy and mod *her* aerial maneuvers map Northern core

rock extinct volcanoes lush with perforations cloak them
suspend them under numbers shadows from another place

·

—or site : the Emerald Viewer marks an avatar invisible
as it visits strolls beneath the lindens the lime honey bracts

in the log-on Lab World structured from permissions where
who hangs at your space from your space's erased from you

nor can you take your own movement for granted
earth and physics afterthought (interface) you install

an IM app in your dream equip folding but unfading
tutelary mesmerie with chat while *falling* as a peregrine

tinsel buttercup foil painted roof ruined roof of the Plaza
verdigris mansard copper slate rushing toward her she could tell

by a tension in the air wire-fine overhead—one rustling
shift—time to be swept back to sea so typed in mistakenly

(no peregrine eye) randomly assigned CAPTCHA squiggle
Turing° test box of twisted-letter text to tag her

                                        personhood denied

CCD   a way-to-see device unrelated to sight
lens-less emulsion-less blind as Homer°

it counts and remembers counts and remembers

subdivision silicon chip pixel wells.
kick out electrons : at the end of each exposure

a grid of numbers an array to catch brightness

emulsion takes down 1 in a 100 photons : 1
CCD : 90   *mehr Licht* more Light Big Bang

radiation residue every ray from radio to gamma

post-persons' fast cheap out-of-control
probe-less pen-less visionless light

pouring in / kicking out

AND of course it is
a wave a sound broken into bits
threaded through numbers

you will take me to mean
nautiline spirals
Florentine chapels Doric temples
al-Hambran Taj Mahalian
symmetries Persian figures

or will you understand it as
the undecidability
between code and capital
the immaterial bio-economy
essence of bio-information
packaged in crystal hint of jasmine

no you are a fancier of stars
you think Arecibo mega array
the billionsfold
data re-splayed quintillionfold

or eyes forward you mention
video macro attractors CNN
blog minis all pull all
seduction neural icon
image flux the real

RARA AVIS

telepresence installation by Eduardo Kac°

not the old vicarial
            Holy Communion
nor the older
            surgery
            pregnancy
            sex
instead
            another newer way to enter each other to share
            the same
            (telematic) co-ordinates
to share
            via circuitry and hardware (these
            vary) surveillance an ambience physical robots and avatars
wander
the augmented body invaded hosts
            ping body
            composite unfragmented neither
            all-here not all-there sliding in
            shifts
the viewer is transported into the aviary
            and sees from the pov of the *Macowl* a telerobotic tropical
            (eyes front so owl) macaw (C·C·D camera eyes)
Voilà! space instanter Virtual
            connected through the Net
            as well remote
participants share owl's body
            vicarially in and out of the macaw
            other birds in the aviary (flying) 'real'
                        though for them too this is negotiated
locals :: remotes animals :: telerobots
for sale

10

freeware gets a grayscale
commercial product color
color feed to multicast frame rates available to still fewer
profession older than the oldest
vicarial lure vampiric pull past skin body in body

STEEL brace five inch wide or smaller with radius
corners clamps left rib to right perduring but prior

glimpse big black bra both silk and industrial
substantial armor below the breasts

view of lorgnette eye mask black and their analogy

at one point tightening all along that band
seemed to thicken and expand into a whole

set of black constructivist Gabo° but no Nevelson°
wheeling stage extruded arc topology

complicated nutcracking space-through-space

to breathe around the ends of it seemed possible
as if it would stay there but the ribs move away

as if they withdrew contracting even further
from the nails or screws into a silk djellaba

then this very swift appearance of diffused

low light from the center of that line
purple-blue illumining pebble strewn bleak

barren moonscape nothing organic
a sense of such release such rightness

and I fell asleep

OPENING hands of clock time ∨ ← see
already say fly! migration! virtual event!
lightcone ten-ten plot digitized spot pixels
far from steeple bells their wave≈≈sound≈≈

or *not* : master-church slave-monk obedient
cipher scriptor in a cell executing tone
by rope (1010 is 10 in binary—a semi-
extraneous sidebar (inline) here)

ALGORITHM

Recipe

Ingredients   *Instructions*

instructions   map a metaphor or more
                                 to computational processes (not
                                            to *compositional*
                                                    capiche?)

                                 twiddle (de dee) tweak (de dum)
                                 execute / run   repeat
                                 till well (enough)

                                 done oh
                                 will this one
                                 halt

MEASURABLE pleasures
30 seconds or so of a non-changing environment
are enough to relax *Octofungi*

             inorganic anemone
                          electro-sensitive to light
whose small arms tip and reach extend and rock

        a plug-in neural net—
its ingredients *mass : atoms*   whereas
                bit packet life

        can transit the solar system in hours its ingredients
instructions—
(only who to receive?
        what storage-and-expression system?)

Whale ancestor coming ashore air-breather mammal
after an eon returned to the ocean—

        Digital biotics well-adapted to space : is this life
going *back* or   moving *on*   escaping
earth and the coils of DNA as the algorist asserts—

Cross it! Jump the bitomic / atomic barrier declared frontier
        the airy cages hacked
           reconfigured   felled   unspared— are we clear?

THE SAME interaction the same charge and enormous

speed my brother Finn° my virtual my transient

twin seething with energy some

or none or any at all

except that one

number that makes me

real and not

him he the ghostly the free

loader the thief exuberant slid in under the bell

UNTIL recently considered not writing
not reading the readme
when all else fails the assailed grid goes down data congeals

>The housekeeper arrives to remove Eryk
>The housekeeper arrives to remove Eryk

canned instructions are not what you (written) need you need
connection type-chat upgrade feeds ping simulate engage
find Easter eggs work the layering zoom

to global and back spun z plied s or
as in ancient
fiber foundry repositories *also binarized* the reverse—

>Everdeen wraps][*.mez°][in electric blanket telepathic controls

positively 3-D
until recently considered not writing (khipu / quipu)
(ascii)(C)

>][*.mez][says, "Sue, 4 1nce I managed 2 sit back & ab.sorb rather
>than prattle on :)"

BIRGITTA° the Healer

and *Graugans* the gray lag goose *Anser*

anser and Babalu-Aye°

(Bab-ilu) gate of God

and the man who listened all the time

Nijinski° (Vaslav) and

orisha Oya° with that bit of buffalo

on her shin yet

and Simone° who did "Fall, gall . . .

and gash gold-vermilion" as Father

Hopkins° saw

—and Mister Rogers° quiet

butt of slurs who knew childhood grit

broadcast engineering nit-

pick knew the only neighborhood we'd

know was mediated magic

knew how knew

why we had to be *inside* it

Sea Dragons

IN that shot they take

on the water at night from a rowboat
moored somewhat south of dead center
light from the moon is older
than light from the trees
light from the lapping
shore's grassy wash older than light
from the fish-jump near their oar
pulled
back on board

a tissue of histories   no snapped shut

moment though light hit lens in an instant
(deferring all stories of where a photon
goes) for the sake of survival
for the sake of passage ease
the sake of cosmic reading
ease ease in
to this none
can
exist *compañera* feel it know no instantaneous

photo   'the whole'   lake

UPSTART stars
of themselves could not (and cannot)
hold it together

their high hung hazy cradle river
cut loose from a time that predates stars
would disappear

fleeing forever from itself in every part
(micro-consequence earth-ending of course
but this is the Big Picture)

ordinary matter (anywhere) too laughably
little to hold it together
a halo

holds it
Milky Way disappearing at an ever faster breakaway speed
unreachable ever were it not for featherweight

traceless twins
or 'hidden dimensions' sounding way too much like
angels

on the head of a pin
I know (don't clone spam or text me
your complaints) how grossly heavy a feather

is
it's a metaphor—
if only

OR the *I Ching*° solid line shifts to broken—or
back a moving line a possible path

along chaotic cell conditions *short* of tsunamic
Huracanic° solitonic—*or not*—William

James° to that earthquake *bring it on!*
(1906 Palo Alto a visiting professor)

die-offs openly welcomed by the one quarter
expecting Jesus to recur here this next year

tolerated by the overwhelmed silver bullet
confusion no solfatara dragon

breath on the neck I crane out my window hear
mason's woodpecker hammer pointing brick

WATER, WATER EVERYWHERE

William Katavalos°
interviewed by Deborah Gans
Bomb 97 Fall 2006

Katavalos—architect whose work I crave—
claims he came to love liquidity via language :
"piss, shit, snot, scum, bile, and puke . . . ."

Why crap and jism, crud, seep, fail this list
derived from Joyce° I can't imagine,
not to mention blood. What he craves, amniotic

incorporation, tunnels, not towers;
hates the surface of the sea, won't swim,
only dive in a bubble-less re-breather.

He requires separation of mass from surface,
mass of liquid, surface plastic,
creating ballooned mesodermal organs

within the body house—skeleton and skin
identifiable, still, but so subordinate so shifting
he jokes "form swallows function," and exults

"the transparency of a mass like water
is like having liquid concrete."
Architect whose work I fear—here, a Mafioso feel.

I do agree, I want more than a box with a door
on it, or a minimized surface; although
so many would be glad for it, content to lose

rooms within rooms onto rooms "you can go
through via apertures, in almost . . . peristaltic
progress" (department stores I can't get out of!)

or Italian towns, or Tiffany's° mansion now
burned down, "a hundred rooms and every [one]
a different organic form." The secret charm,

sudden Hide-and-Seek : lost "[i]n this place
you would wear waterproof
clothing . . . wearable computers, e-broidery . . . ."

He focuses on "*inner* body . . . including the kidneys
. . . the ureters . . . bringing the outside in, it is
the inside, inside out," which, to my mind, undoes

'inner', another non-transformative flip;
yet conduits, "hydroforms—hydrocolumns,
hydroarches, hydrovaults," on paper as seductive

as what he was seduced by, Palladian villas, vacuum
domes, and a quality of light like Lalique, ornamental
complexity, the Sansovino library in Venice,

Debussy's° Engulfed Cathedral, a "Breton
legend . . . the Cathedral of Ys sinks into the sea each day
at sunset, rising again at sunrise with great majesty . . . ."

Pisces without Fire Signs, spacey, I neglect
gravitational grounding, but the air
in motion, the wind tells me the Cathedral of

Is sinks into the sea still shimmering at sunset
maintaining ghost presence, breathing all through
the night (default surveyor stars marking out

sea surface, sometimes storming auroral)
before rising again with the sun, with a majesty I
bring, I accord, awed—but also without me.

"Is Security the Next Aesthetic in Architecture?"
He means not living "in a black box with a bunch
of black boxes, living blind." He means

a house you understand where you can
—yourself—generate power, know how
things are grown (hydroponic), how to fix it;

"architecture of mass that does not have to be
quarried or carried to the site," degrees
of transparency easily changed.

He claims kinship to "The Glass Chain. The crystal
house becomes the liquid house," he says,
and says light penetrating stained

glass without puncture instructs on virgin
birth. He is asserting muliebrity. He's right about
calling on mathematics, "like using a ten-ton press

to crack a walnut," but has become obsessed
with Feynman's° obsession, 243; his own,
761; and 100.115.965.22, the anomalous

magnetic moment of the electron, most thoroughly
verified, carefully measured in the history
of physics— He engages blocks of numbers,

begins to predict numeric masses flushing from
accelerators : "it's sub-numeral: good for nothing
but describing nature." "It is organic. It is . . . numeric

animation." "Architecture . . . a succession
of gender geometries." He is
a professor : "[the] temple mount was used for

sacrificial surgery." "[A]rchitecturalized"
 as "geometric dentils[,]"
" . . . blood dripping over its edges . . . ."

KEEP it | kill it   *call it!*   up

or down ↓ data warrant data thumb data agency security arts
department *dependency* danger-wrangler in the pit
handicapping on the fly data are not
                                        evidence
                    for that to which they *drownage* attest

            the horse dissolved into monkeys

and the quiet into comatose lady at the mirror
bar late afternoon truthfully there is no noon in the timeless
old hotel cool concentric waves of dulled semicircle silver open
                    sparks shower from the live cage monkeys
            gingerly testing fences in the urban forest

            every junction is a number a corner a vertex

every junction a tone   intervals   swimmingly overlap confines
within the octave Octavia° swallowing mandorla martini
                    glasses of unclouded
            gin in the permadim grotto
of echoing surfaces a faint jade in the beveled edge hint of mint

FUTURE of comprehension

each ignorant of more exponentially more each day each one
ask Googenie it is done
no sooner returned says the Fish (retrieval) piling on
privation's narrowing local unimodal
niche traps

> *door banging at its twisted hinge*

resisted : global category schemes
fallout focus on the simpler the shorter collectively
dyslexic (kids) unable *fill in the blank* to read the (eroding)
writing on the (Corps of Army Engineering
levee) wall

> *rust filigree iron*

1st-order detritus bouncing alone in systems or as networks
how my being crushed is just
avoided by your being torn apart my compression your
tension collapse 'musically' averted intertransforming islands
modulating bodies

pleading

my wish Genie—jump to questions beyond my current ken
Fish I ask that you not send me home so soon
to my insatiable hovel Basket Buoy hold the oceans Watery
Ball I cling to the birdcage as it falls and fills and empties it is
an aerial

CHORAL quarantine of curiosity
                              Eve°   Persephone°
broken by sea by dyke destruction

reassignment male sailors faring forth to murder
first to gold and god glory and the queens' ambition
beyond pillows of Hercules°

                              the goal
fantasia course by compass to hold—
a hemorrhagic current fouls the archipelagoes

OVERLAY lady made of printed blue ruffled curtain stuff
on a lofty scale bending across
and letting down into the scene a baby it seems in a blue shawl

wall of thundercloud transforming headdress
thick-fingered branch-hand matted sky deep yellow
storm surge caught in its trident

white head whitehaired polar bear skin clad
explorer glistening fur imploring her by silent
splash ice shelf floe & slab buckled slush broken off

I FORGOT I can forget because *I'm* not *I'm*
networked-support and invention*
servant / artifact / prosthesis / bare hand : Greek scorn

category includes women even unworked-out bodies
(a slightly different story) while to navigate Pacifically's
to wait for the island to arrive beside you

staying selfstill the flow of course coursing away
Forrest Gump° cargo cult the other other side
of that I forgot and so I move ahead unknowing and can't stop

---

* *O* at least a *soupçon* of evolutional Darwinian°
the neural the nucleic acid the tool not *aids* to memory
m'am *memory itself* where's the brain that executes

code in its pan ahead of time not just writes it and runs
it that Promethean° dream in the toilet blame his brother
eco-Eden integrated almost all figured out then Epimetheus°

forgot—adrift the Ur dream uterine rocking or roving are we
part of a chain of many chains of a family that includes
heavy metal-maker uncles : adolescent pop stars

diatoms extremophiles wolves few and disappointing
cousinage answers from fishes plants or wolf-raised human
children loosed cannon man man   in particular

because I forgot atoll / rim-shot / fire / flood / black gold /
platform / pipes / pills / protocols / pings got different too fast don't
traditionals every*any*where (if such exist) attest live this

reproach—songline you lost it you dropped it let the ball slide
from your hand fall—to us my grandfather could fix a buggy and a jet
not a computer but that my dad did

do and then I forgot I can forget because
I'm not : all support adoption invention *Dichtung*
connection *techne* flow *imago* schooner can't get off

32

Comely Substitutions

Gibbs° gifted Maxwell° with a plaster cast
the size of a fist. Locked in its grip

each & every history of water; the cast, a grandsire
node on the traceroute of legible images of total time.

Talan° made a movie, nipple tree of Nowhere, *Ingenstans,*
Sweden's riverbank where the children drowned,

children run over by a boat—by a bot. Why seek
to tell them apart (children and *bots*) reliably

or fast? To keep polls (clicks) unpolluted, discount
ersatz million hits. People suck at this, too slow,

run over; so, yes, an automatic application : you play,
it gets smarter. Talan cites Duchamp°, *Network of Stoppages.*

•

Cortical CPU network body—angled upon it, slices
and shadows, assembled, loom by torchlight; comely

substitutions, cool, as-if-new, code-views expose-
distort, as they blow up, manifolded-ness-entanglement.

Jeremy's°, volumetric; Talan urges tesseractic. No more!
Reverse-engineering 'nature'? Nature, please, is Disney°—

Reverse instead reverse-engineering's computational
feat—or drive it forward, for we tire, conscious

choice, of the sea on fire—we cannot chance
that the oil would stop without it, without *simulation*.

The deep water drilling didn't *start* without one.
Apocalypse, how long? Eleven-million years or so

ago, sonar probes, ping-echoing easy-pass dolphin bands
began to sentinel-haunt, to test, to re-shape the coasts.

Hunger Dragon of Unstable Ruin

TECHNICIANS in blue collarless jumpsuits trained
at DeVry or State (or where exactly?) penetrate my body

so fully open to their target beams mediated by non-
diaphanous machines from Siemens or GE a hardware

almost old school though not so old as robbed graves
anatomy artist charts note bio-parts futures actively

traded today too new school stem cell deals having not gone
down yet even they passé the aim the blood brain barrier

mania to replace that wet vision engine map flesh out of
flesh for this technicians in white three-quarter

coats trained at MIT Harvard or Somewhere Institutes
visit the splayed plasticized donated Bodies exhibit

with a somewhat antiquarian interest (offensive as it
is to fundamentalists of all stripes who avow

the body's importance near death if not in life—
whitecoats know better shuffling mindset on the hiPod)

DEER have swollen in the freight car filling
it   in the pickup slung across
the back

seat swell burst pitching
forward over driver's eyes hooves nick
the screen the GPS

they have
become a nuisance you know
not held in check

TWO dragons
keep a pearl
        in the air untouched
if yes then no if no then yes

untouchable between them
sustained between them
                    perhaps
the flow of air

each guarded by nine more
rampant
        ready
should one falter perhaps

at long
        last
able to
withdraw untouched

into stones to function there
mapped by slow
domain
if no then yes if yes then no

VARIETIES of ecocide : does it matter
text 30001

viral vs. nuclear warheads :
answers at 10

we hear from gamers math professor
simulators those in actual rehearsal

involuntary
immersion in the real : a pharmal

target each blockbuster drug
to reach each until

it goes off-patent
factoid : leeches make shocking comeback

VANISHING moist glade a dump of readymades
you can get for a song for happening upon it

posting the land declaring it abandoned
along with the sea ready for reframing

ready for transpackaging unit payload trove
hold *biológico químico* superducer *mojo*

NOT
how to form but how to *feel*
—and *feed*—that
shift
  how

long
  after Big Tiamat° Bang how early on
did that *was*
that
  emergence of life

swarm
Tiamat
  torn by your sons wrestled down
how long
  before

  the gang move
  back to
how to
  form
  9 eons 10 moons

GREAT Pan° is dead
the projection withdrawn damp
leatherclad greenmen melt into the woods

    (idolizing idle incubus's
incubation idyll isolated Individual
      infatuates itself)

black-boxable the hoaxable
soul of Samson°
hacked

NOTHING to fence or to bank
nothing to unveil or reveal or to save

      even while feeling the violence pile up
      inside petty or other

nothing to read
      petty or bloody

no well
no womb no replenishing silo left unbroken

      none unpoisoned

              even as violence
      re-arrives

even now moist
iris *ayahuasca* Arabians racing

ethical resistance to enlisting brine shrimp

      koto duet with bee

heirloom seed
a screen tuned to snow

SILENT compact smooth stone longing to split
cleanly open all silver mica black
gleaming chip schematic surface

unbudging rock pulse suddenly ragged
sworn to a tip tall scrawny mountain tower
transceiving tines atop bony fire

now a padded package
opening to spill gores of silk
crumpled moths falling from the parachute

VAGARY
face of faun doeskin spine
all my as
her body doe
in soaking silence
Merton's
rain
drenching the thick mulch
. . . filling the gullies
and crannies of the wood . . .

washing out the places
where men have stripped . . .
the most comforting speech
in the world, the talk
that rain makes by itself
all over the ridges . . . .
Nobody started it, nobody
is going to stop it. It will
talk as long
as it wants, the rain.

—Thomas Merton°
Raids on the Unspeakable

Dragon Maps

EVERYONE knows that dragons don't exist. But while this simplistic formulation may satisfy the layman, it does not suffice for the scientific mind . . . .

Cerebron, attacking the problem analytically, discovered three distinct kinds of dragon : the mythical, the chimerical, and the purely hypothetical. They were all, one might say, nonexistent, but each nonexisted in an entirely different way . . . .

Suppose, for example, one organizes a hunt for such a dragon, surrounds it, closes in, beating the brush. The circle of sportsmen, their weapons cocked and ready, finds only a burned patch of earth and an unmistakable smell : the dragon, seeing itself cornered, has slipped from real to configurational space.

—Stanislaw Lem°, *The Cyberiad*

SUBJECT: [webartery] Short Graphism
From: "Alan Sondheim°" <sondheim@panix.com>
Date: Fri, June 9, 2006 2:58 am

To: webartery@yahoogroups.com
Priority: Normal

Infinitely thin projective slice of difficult equation. The compression
comes to grip[s] with it. There may be shadows of the future, I don't
know . . . coordinates are always variable. When the space
moves, the[y] become ill. Don't they?

Elsewhere, the real renders. Here it has already given up.

http://www.asondheim.org/graph10.mov
http://www.asondheim.org/graph20.mov

NEWFANGLENESS

after quantum mechanics

> Nature went straight
> all the possible states of any physical
> object formed a linear space

after Gödel°

> archipelagoes of structure
> fen full weedy fertile inexhaustible pod
> of mathematical flowers

after Schrödinger°

> a technical trick sharply
> stressed by many engineered tests became her 'truth'—
> Nature's sewing kit seen stocked with negative roots

after Weyl°

> gauge invariance expands Conservation
> but after Weyl dies enter the lists other
> C sisters Chaos Computation

after Yang°

> asymmetry rules
> unruly interactions between forming fields
> unique

this kind of link

> —or allegory—or rigorous raft
> first : coordinates & fluxions & symbolic logic
> second : cut-and-seam-glued Riemannian° surface

third : twinned towers

across—or between—number theory *&* physics!
now : quantization of mathematics
now : deep equivalence

what sort of (t)rope is this?

RUPTURE is complete with the CD
photons abrade no mass
no scragnail stylus scraping a groove
emancipation of memory from touch has been fulfilled

capture complete : whatever the sun
looks like it's doing it's not (moving) only
witches or old wives connect by look
man-shaped mandrake root

deep connection is unseen by (unseen) rules
protocols seeds : only some
evolve a feel—that wizard René Thom°—
for how rules live or for what lives in *them* as

emergent as appearing after all tightly seamed
to seeming ground ruling in its rolling is
best of breed code executing while
light show crowds exchange shot|shot|shot dream

Are you kidding? Quarks, too, can *choose?*
     Conway° and Kochen°, old dragons, well
vetted, claim—no—prove, if given a free hand to choose

     their gear direction while quizzing quarks with questions,
       taking their measure, then, too, whim-

driven *&* not determined, a particle's response. To be
     precise—*the universe's response near* the particle un-
determined by the Whole prior history of World Time *&* Space.

     In fairness, it's the theory's 'strong'
       (min, spin, twin) form—could they claim more?

Imagine haranguing electrons,
     just say no—
Imagine addressing zoomers *sans* apparatus. Up and at it,

     again, are you, pairs of them grumble, maybe even hiss;
       gauging us, too, in their stinging way.

WITH numbers I am led into depths of
God the Seeress said but the gnomes

warned Brouwer° to limit himself
to Protestant numbers not to say Puritan

to avoid Tibetan baroque epicyclic
generative numbers spilling on the ground like spores

or mushrooms springing after rain—
the gnomes gave stricter sparser instructions

but particles it seems no followers of Ockham°
Catholic breeders idols & icons bent on immolation

what trajectories! what jets! what missing mass
tight curly fleece of lamb released

wiry wild ecstatic rolling
per-existing that's what the numbers said

some *things* (tetrahedral) consist altogether of

4	corners
4	faces
6	edges
12	angles
1	insideness
1	outsideness
1	concavity
1	convexity
2	poles of spinnability

    ──

32	features

behavioral potential

        axial rotation
        orbital travel

        expansion-contraction
        torque (axial twist)

        inside-outing (involuting-evoluting)
        precession (axial tilt)

        interprecessionings among plural systems
        self-steering of a system (precessionally done)

some *powers* are only otherness-viewable
        some only multi-otherness-realizable

        ". . . not until a six
        otherness appears remotely, approaches, and associates
        with the fivefold system can the latter learn
        from the newcomer of its remote
        witnessing that the fivefold
        system has indeed
        been *rotating*
        axially . . ."

VRTA° the Dragon not letting exist that which longs to exist
Vrta Circle Serpent sliding analog

octave cut to pieces
every battle

oooooo

on the 1st
day   the day of 1st division

of spherific creation
Vrta wanded all Universe with 6-bladed tongue

at a stroke

she separated all events outside her chosen system (1)
from all events (2) inside her system segregating with *horizons*

(3) non-simultaneous remote unreachable prior
events from (4) all *ditto* subsequent

events from of course all those encoding (5)
the garden &

(6) those occurring
synchronously or coincidentally to

and with her darling
garden events

social news of which has preoccupied perhaps unwisely the millennia

catastrophic forms and safepaths

fold	*cusp*	*swallowtail*	*butterfly*	*hyperbolic umbilic*	*elliptic umbilic*	*parabolic umbilic*
be	become	agitate	give	crest	penetrate	eject
end	separate	split	send	collapse	pierce	lance
begin	unite	knit	receive	cover	annihilate	link
when	*where*	*which*	*how*	*what*	*who*	*why*
TIME	PLACE	DISTINCTION	MOTION	TAXONOMY	IDENTITY	AUSPICIOUSNESS
edge all-or-none	fault transition	slit crack	pocket shell	arch wave	needle hair	weather fountain

flows   cascades   iterations

$v = x^3$	*fold*
$v = x^4$	*cusp*
$v = x^5$	*swallowtail*
$v = x^6$	*butterfly*
$v = x^3 + y^3$	*hyperbolic umbilic*
$v = x^3 - 3xy^2$	*elliptic umbilic*
$v = x^2 y + y^4$	*parabolic umbilic*

NEBEN° and *Nach*° *Einander* known
as Nevin and Nick (or Knock—
Knock being the enforcer or more
benignly the manager
of meaning seemingly except
that Nevin the touchy feelingly
planned parties and sitting
settings preferring round tables)
are brother colluder orderers : a pox
on both their one houses

a cognitive flow field (around one known shape)
might be mapped (onto the flow field) around one of *the seven*

|

questions : conformality (e.g. *why* and a goblet)
conformal mapping notably makes use of complex variables (applet)

|

preserving the angles—cascades of *how*
vigilance required for higher twistedness (skateboarding)

ζ

"*when* answered: 'Because messenger-RNA duplicates information from
the DNA spiral and turns to ribosomes, *where* proteins are synthesized

|

. . . ,'" he prompted asked "'*When? How* does it know *when? How* does it
switch from one state to another? Following *what* roads? *Where* is the map?'"

|

some are extra ? dimensions 'games people play' meditation psychosis
'winning ways' sex and chemo-direct mushroom grape cactus (chocolate)

|

mathematical germs (critical points) of the catastrophe geometries frame
change with stability—love stability equivalence typicality isotropy (more)

ζ

up to 4
control factors and 2
behavior axes there are only 7

but where the sum of control (slow) and state (fast) dimensions equals 11
there are 11

for dimensions greater than 5
in the control space and 2
in the state (active / behavior) space *the number of catastrophes is infinite*

1 control 1 state   *fold*   (more | applet)

      origami : mountain / valley

2 control 1 state   *cusp*   (more | applet)

      origami : reverse

3 control 1 state   *swallowtail*   (more | applet)

      origami : double reverse

4 control 1 state   *butterfly*

               containing a 'pocket'
               of compromise
               with a surface in 4D   (more | applet)

      origami : triangular sink fold

3 control 2 state   *elliptic umbilic*   (more | applet)

                       or

3 control 2 state   *hyperbolic umbilic* (more | applet)

               triangle immersed in a saddle-shaped plane
               playing insies and outsies off we go to Ithaca
               to petition *Whom?* Daina Taimina° to crochet it
               swerve to visit surfers who inhabit wavebreak

4 control 2 state   *parabolic umbilic*   (more | 2 applets)

        to glimpse in slice or projection at a calligraphic
             stroke a cup swirling its wine
                a funneling
                  goblet
                   a
                 chalice
            enclosing and probably
         sucking a mineral-rich mushroom

so it comes in the fullness of mind and it came to
pass to collapse the column *columns begone*
a central sanctum cleared covered by a dome
well first one arch two then a few intersecting
high heavenly span if the dome were inverted
should it become some huge dish
what pulls it together would pull it apart
if it could be placed in orbit it would drift apart
a chain is used around the dome of St. Peter's in Rome

a chain is used around the dome of St. Peter's in Rome
if it could be placed in orbit it would drift apart
what pulls it together would pull it apart
should it become some huge dish
high heavenly span if the dome were inverted
well first one arch two then a few intersecting
a central sanctum cleared covered by a dome
pass to collapse the column *columns begone*
so it comes in the fullness of mind and it came to

GROTHENDIECK°
sees everything globally from the beginning Hironaka°
                    said *no coordinates no*
        equations

roller coasters have no sudden on
        a dime
change of direction however steep
                no cusp
                no crossing through themselves—

        their shadows do : sharp projections of the smooth

pulling back
        to the smooth
from tangle   local
                tumult disappears : only *global*   lift
left

inside the crush cross point so multifarious—a many nenny
whorled

blow   it up (gentle difficult
balloon work) make it
smooth

YES Jane it is regrettable that the mathematical
with so much to offer
by way of reframing should be in thrall
to such a degree to the defense & security retrenchment
agenda complete with strong support
for money-changers
the field's heavy lifting toward promotion of some singular
global threat—say terrorism decrypted—or
exploration of space
after the bombing stops : an Archimedean°
precedent
http://www.google.com/search?hl=en&rls=GGLD,GGLD:2005-
05,GGLD:en&sa=X&oi=spell&resnum=0&ct=result&cd=1&q=Grothendieck+
mathematics&spell=1 Grothendieck
like Bartleby°
refused

CATASTROPHIC FORMS AND SAFEPATHS

1 : when
it ends no scrambling back up over that *fold*

2 : where to intervene
to find a path from the *cusp* to get back to the green

3 : which emergent slit
stabilities surround *swallowtail* instabilities

4 : a butterfly hovers it's a *swallowtail*
with extra control *how* does
Xin Wei° choose Chinese or Italian or English to speak now

5 : teasingly dumb light show optics
in the focal surfaces reflecting Turrell° if as in an ancient
culture our kiva placed our chalice calyxical
spaces could be our every room
cloud gathering light slow meticulous lingering imposing
baseline crystal information
what boundaries *what* nomenclature patterns *hyperumbilic*
typology taxonomy centered on one (focal
point) or the other complementarily
mapping self to shadow see[d]ing with two eyes
polarized perspectives twistedness twee-ing

6 : elliptiumb
kith kin kind kabuki killer
impersonator danger needle hair fluid *who*
she was her obit known not knew not all that while
caught in the headlight
all relegate to market therapeutic celebritic
backscattering and twinkling and blurring

whose whom
my home a summing
two foci me alone me together shifting
flute body an implicit question
holes open close

7 : *why*

the focal point
          questioner locus

the vertex equidistant
          between focus and directrix

the *linea directrix*
          basal line below two units

from the focus
          where I stand

the axis of reflective symmetry
          goes through me to that line

intersecting the vertex
          nadir of the upturned curve

every point on the curve falls plumb to the directrix
          traveling as far as it would come to come to me

orientation cup upheld or goblet grounded
          thrown down Hamlet°

upended overturned unfillable Hamlet
       wants unfillable *why*

parabola's ellipse one focus at infinity
        inverse transform of a cardioid

baseball in the air without the air
        parabolic umbilic

neither
      is there any ball

∞ INFINITE ways to change continuously lapping licking staying
at (near) equilibrium

7 but   seven stable ways to change abruptly   *jump*
Hell's kitchen smoke plume fire cat
something's got to give it *duh*
does . . . spectacular
collapse
        . . . or the baby's nap . . . unfolding

stably disappearing stability a
ha downdraft snowflake oh also snow
ball rolling into mind soot chippiness ice

utter irrelevance
        scale | laws | causes | radiation
to the form to
        the gliding shape the wind the word the (class 4)
computation

MY teams were
Penrose° vs. Prigogine°
Brouwer° vs. Bohr°
and the oddity of
Clerk Maxwell° or
Max Planck° not standing for
in the end what they
discovered
imagined surfaced
their deep implicits
tolerable first as problem
con[in]struc[tui]tions
but as the house whole
the pier the ur-gravel
harsh

ONE and another *oaa*
one another *oa*
yin yang *yy*
no *y* without *yy*
no *o* without *oa*
no negative is *not* virtual

negative is other to another *o* to *a*
negative is mirror image
so widely seen so widely mis-seen
as opposite while facing
inside
out *io*

io of *oa*
easiest done
with a glove to do to see from 3-
D
oa io
old McMaxwell° had

super secondary symmetries
pairing into spin poles of secondary vertices
produced by the complex secondary

crossings of *oa   oaa*

Alive Inside the Dragons

LINES spears nets knots have-knots
                                            no-horse

they are not here
                            they are straddling sand sky peer wait
for wind
            shift manhigh water python tunnel to span
swallow mansea creature ocean deepest pounding breath
                        sea surface scumble sullen south
wind bitter flat as for with Easter
                                    Island they wait forward

they are not here with us thus we see we are
not here the smallness
                        of us
refugee camp concert audience collapsed
towers no prior us constituted thus
                                        seconds in seconds

dream of we
            a garden's worth of marigold bluebell creatures in the lily
trumpets tubes
                                    radio cities

Duke° a hundred years ago stood up on the 'bluebird' the cataclysmic
wave the spawn the lethal avalanche
                        from Diamond Head to the Harbor
1.75 miles my
                    back in collapse not a duke not a sleek invention not a
            kayak not a wave
                        flotsam kelpish
alignment alone thrust position on the wall averts wipeout

the tatting aunt bore to her grave for want
of a human relay
                    vital connection correct protocol
transmission fear of dissipation dissolution drizzle lethal
error
                    wordhoard treasure   here be dragons rather
die
         a wooden barb may be parried but a verbal barb cannot
         he tao rakau e taea te karo, he tao kupu e kore e taea te karo

using a fishhook made from the jawbone
of her grandmother no-horse

GIRL without hands

      falls into drivenness akimbo
      her silver prostheses held under running
      water a mirror
      slide dazzle of drops and prisms
      held underneath the fountain
      transmit to her questioning held out
      cheek their coldness

handless and fearless

      grain in the grave
      wave in the wine
      gauginos
      sequestered or combined with everything
      the bulk the branes the virtual
      deep the kitchen sink
      hole hanging
      out
      to dry dripping newborn diamond
      drops of mass

INDIGO maroon purple Tyrant
gorged to menstrual black

the only Towel pastel cool pale small
thin linen pink slim banding

of handwork tatting or bobbin not
point lace a border ecru

modest bits of inset scroll
or hemstitch not *opus anglicanum*

yet very finely woven jacquard° figured
barely discernible pattern on pattern

HER tidings cascades of lightning deathpools and lace
semaphore dysphorias continuance *creation*
although some attempt to construct by closing in on

staking names ever narrower names ever newly discrepant

her choices sequences many languageless intuited
before offered up to loquacity and simbiltons

continual   contingent   her continuo

AS MUCH contingency as craft
Longyearbyen Doomsday Ark
seed vault on Svalbard

going *on* is the enormous
thing I do Agnes not
forward first an eschewed

then an indefinable now almost
inexistent direction but
dimensions abound we stipulate

three (it feels small) million
seeds Agnes in the desert
Martin° mostly alone said

MEDIUM of cloth deep in Chelsea Storage tomb vaults
Manhattan Afrikan market every day busy
bloom of dress and headdress

Inkan records of state tactile triply
dimensional writings with knot bulk knot twist knot
ply not penned images

graphemes or screens the cellular register : innards
molecular model the cords' code working in pairs
one a program execution re-*cording*

simulations statistics census
polycyclical scheduling even—can it be?—histories
Quipucamayoc° computation

tunes "a data-dense medium whose clarity did not depend on
expansion into words"
Inkan road system larger than Rome's

"life had to be lived like a khipu"
khipus map features of social life not language
language writers speculate

what headdress for Carrie Brezine° weaver mathematician
ethnographer creator of the *Khipu Database*
she is studying especially skirt borders and intersecting warps

Beatrix Potter°
proffered "exquisite drawings" and her discovery
—*symbio[n]tic* mycology—
in her paper
(1897)
"Germination of the spores of *Agaricineae*"

a voice unseen
unseeable at Kew requisitely
male
eschewed "unnatural union
between a captive Algal damsel and a tyrant
Fungal master"

Beatrix Potter
"It is extraordinary how botanists have . . . not in the least
seen the broad bearing of it."

Beatrix Potter
"I was not shy, not at all. I had it up and down
with him.
His line was on
the outside of civil . . . . I informed
him

that it would all be in the books in ten years, whether
or no,
and departed giggling.
I ought to wear
blue
spectacles on these occasions."

4 ARE simple

    being

          beginning

                              ending

      changing

1 2 complex

    capturing and *sending* it on I *crossed*
    the river I *almost* did *fastening* to
    shore and *giving* myself time *rejecting* more
    effort *failing* to emerge *taking* hold of reeds
    and kelp *stirring* my feet
    emitting streams of breath *cutting* those off

domains bounded
by catastrophic spaces in every described
process are the privileged actants

each contracted to a point
by text they come in contact
in a region contracted

to a point itself by text
so to each *process*
a *graphic*

belonging to one
(*interaction* morphology)
1 of 1 6

IN-DIVISIBLE plays X-streame dial with her cousin
indi-vidual who thinks he's the older

indivi-dual probes indivisi-ble as if in play click
no respecter of gender age or any other indiVisi murmurs

dear cousine envelope this enclosure this unopenable
me for tempus flees and our god does not repeat

whoa no he says we are riddled with bugs trapped in gaps
I am gathering fast the past in particulate skipping rifts

you'll gasp my art my stats my legality post processing
dear cuz surcease click artifactuals attentively

touch you can but not track down my eventeffect
my singuvocalocity no less entangledly yours

DELICACY of the ghost creatures

from it seems a damp cave

walking stick water striders harp

speed warped feet

as if newly unchrysalised

no wings

they are walking a nucleus

massed and several outliers

along a curved path

the horse's name is not Chestnut

Ruth's° eyes are closed not green

does she know Niobe°

there is a zombie at the wheel
who finds acceptable all risk

(his flesh looks like mine)

a crinkle monkey in the swamp
mind tricky and brisk

(his moves feel like mine)

headless mannequin draped
white print snakeskin dress

(pale fakery filling me with dread)

a boneless man used up
by apparatchik juggernaut

(scrivener like me)

the one who hoped to poach
cockroach strategy adrift

(like me time-amnesic overreaching)

cord-cut all   beyond the call
to heal or heel   *fold   molt*

(wormhole crush crash course)

YOU already know what to do

I sigh untense my feet
I am grateful to the universe for
this reprieve

says the cult narrative

I freeze I see I am
its secret admirer
Armageddon clean slate

restive tugging at
its halter how
instantly

it hits—

fleeting
as ripples flowing off the rim of a clam's
fleshy foot body probingly slowly extending onto shifting

sand I

in the unclear
quiet
wait

INVOKING Tzimtzum° Persephone° contracted Peirce°
                              pure zero
Lucretian° swerves plummet Peirce purse zero
failed Puritan American so
                        infinitely
kind to your unmarried wife tinkerer mensch αlpha
                Indus ωmega   hoofwork
script Thirdness diagram numbers
                              and
you nether Ereshkigal° mimophonic
every dawn every dusk pour me out on the sand
        sluice my letters from the slate

°*Codemakers*

Al-Farabi   10th c. mathematician, musician, philosopher; studied in Baghdad

Archimedes   3rd c. BCE fount of mathematics; though himself disinterested in his military 'toys', most famous in his time for these original weapons of terror

Babalu-Aye   god of illness and healing in Yoruba mythology; worshipped in Brazil and the Caribbean

Bartleby   see Herman Melville's "Bartleby the Scrivener: A Story of Wall Street"

Birgitta   Swedish for Brigit, Brighid, Brigantia, Bride; patron of healing, smithcraft, queenship

Bohr, Niels   philosopher-physicist from Copenhagen, awarded Nobel Prize for foundational work in atomic and quantum physics

Brezine, Carrie   mathematician, weaver; founder with Gary Urton of the Khipu Keeper website

Brouwer, Luitzen Egbertus Jan   mathematician, topologist; developed a view of mathematics as the constructive mental activity of humans (intuitionism); opposed to Hilbert formalism

Celan, Paul   Romanian-Jewish concentration camp survivor and suicide, major German-language poet

Conway, John Horton   mathematician; devised the cellular automaton, 'Game of Life'; co-wrote "The Strong Free Will Theorem," *Notices of the American Mathematical Society,* v.56 n.2, 2009, proving that elementary particles must be free to choose their spins in order to make their measurements consistent with physical law

Darwin, Charles   naturalist, game-changer extraordinaire; wrote *On the Origin of Species,* 1859

Debussy, Claude   established a new concept of tonality in European music, wrote *La mer* 1903–1905

Disney, Walt   film producer, showman, innovative animator, creator of Mickey Mouse and theme parks

Duchamp, Marcel   French artist; in 1914 superposed two drawings and a painting to make *Network of Stoppages*

Duke   Duke Kahanamoku, 1890–1968; Olympic swim champion, legendary surfer: "I soared and glided, drifted and sideslipped, with that blending of flying and sailing . . ."

Epimetheus   according to Plato, the one of the twin Titans entrusted with distributing positive traits among the newly-created animals; he forgot to save a trait for man, who is therefore malleably formed by his cultures and technologies; see Bernard Stiegler, *Technics and Time, 1: The Fault of Epimetheus*

Ereshkigal   "great lady under earth," Sumerian-Akkadian goddess of the underworld, Ishtar's older sister

Eve   a woman who wanted to know; Genesis 3:20: "And Adam called his wife's name Eve; because she was the mother of all living," a title previously held by Babylonian Tiamat

Feynman, Richard   Nobelist in physics, popular teacher; developed path integral method from an idea of Paul Dirac's, himself a prior physics Nobelist

Finn   quantum particles (the constituents of existence) have twin particles located elsewhere; I have personified a companion virtual twin as Finn

Forrest Gump   film character; embodies (especially, blissful) ignorance as a powerful constructive tool

Gabo, Naum   Russian-born American Constructivist sculptor

Gibbs, Josiah Willard   first mathematical physicist in the United States; deviser of theoretical foundations for chemical thermodynamics and physical chemistry, inventor of vector analysis; many Nobelists cite his influence

Gödel, Kurt   20th c. logician; his work caused an upheaval in the foundations of mathematics

Grothendieck, Alexander   Fields Medal mathematician, visionary, radical, topologist

Hamlet   a man who dithered; protagonist of Shakespeare's *The Tragical History of Hamlet, Prince of Denmark*

Hendrix, Jimi   rock guitarist who made use of Marshall vacuum tube—not solid state—amplifiers, allowing him to master the use of feedback as a musical effect

Hercules (Pillars of)   promontories flanking the Straits of Gibraltrar; for Europeans to colonize other lands involved securing navigation by learning to determine longitude, which in turn required an accurate seagoing timekeeper, perfected over 40 years by John Harrison, carpenter—a task Isaac Newton thought impossible; see Dava Sobel's account in *Longitude*

Hironaka, Heisuke   algebraic geometer

Homer   oldest oral Greek collective poet, pictured as singular, pictured as blind

Hopkins, Gerard Manley   poet; wrote "Binsey Poplars," "The Windhover: To Christ our Lord"

Huracan[ic]   Mayan wind, storm and fire god who participated in all three attempts at creating humanity; the Taínos, a Caribbean people speaking Arawakan, are the source of many words which appear in Spanish and English, among them *canoa* (canoe), *tabaco* (tobacco) and *Huracan* (hurricane)

I Ching   or   **Book of Changes**   ancient Chinese divination text: each oracle is associated with one of 64 hexagrams (sets of 6 stacked lines, each line specified as either broken or unbroken)

jacquard   fabric woven on a jacquard loom, the first programmable loom; invented by **Joseph-Marie Jacquard** in 1801, it later inspired the computer technology of punch cards

James, William   psychologist, philosopher, teacher of W.E.B. Du Bois and Gertrude Stein; Peirce's one great friend

Jeremy   is **Jeremy Douglass**   digital text artist and software researcher

Joyce, James   influential Irish writer who relished describing body parts and function, see *Ulysses*

Kac, Eduardo poet and multimodal artist; "*Rara Avis* is an interactive telepresence work in which local and remote participants experienced a large aviary with 30 birds from the point of view of a telerobotic macaw"

Katavalos, William professor in the School of Architecture and co-director of the Center for Experimental Structures at Pratt Institute where liquid architecture was developed

Kochen, Simon mathematician; developed Kochen-Specker Paradox; co-wrote "The Strong Free Will Theorem," *Notices of the American Mathematical Society,* v.56 n.2, 2009

Lem, Stanislaw Polish science fiction writer; in WWII active in the Resistance

Lucretius Roman writer; his poem, *On the Nature of the Universe*, advocated a *clinamen* or atomic 'swerve' to embed free will in his materialist, mechanistic, atomic system

Martin, Agnes painter of abstract expressionist visionary grids

Maxwell, James Clerk mathematician and physicist; produced in Maxwell's equations "the most profound and the most fruitful [work] that physics has experienced since the time of Newton" —A. Einstein

Merton, Thomas poet, Trappist monk, social activist

mez (Mary Anne Breeze) writer long involved with networked online communication, virtual game worlds, language modification; quoted here in a snippet of MOO conversation with Eryk, Everdeen, and Sue

nacheinander German adverb, one after the other, in sequence: ranked, hierarchic, asymmetric

nebeneinander German adverb, one next to the other, side by side: egalitarian, connected horizontally

Nevelson, Louise Russian-born American abstract expressionist sculptor

Nijinski, Vaslav Russian ballet dancer and choreographer of Polish origin

Niobe [nigh O bee] Apollo killed her 7 sons, Artemis her 7 daughters—she turned to stone, weeping

Ockham, William of 14th–15th c. English Franciscan friar and philosopher; Ockham's Razor: always opt for the most parsimonious explanation (also **Occam**)

Octavia personification of octave

Oya Yoruba goddess of wind and lightning who creates hurricanes and tornadoes; see Judith Gleason, *Oya: In Praise of the Goddess*

Pan nature spirit, pagan symbol of life

Peirce, Charles Sanders scientist, logician: "I will now say a few words about what you have called Categories, but for which I prefer the designation Predicaments, and which you have explained as predicates of predicates. That wonderful operation . . . by which we seem to create *entia rationis* that are, nevertheless, sometimes real, furnishes us the means of turning predicates from being signs that we think or think through, into being subjects thought of. We thus think of the thought-sign itself, making it the object of another thought-sign. Thereupon, we can repeat the operation . . . and from these second intentions derive third intentions. Does this series proceed endlessly? *I think not* . . . I will only say that . . . the divisions so obtained must not be confounded with the different Modes of Being: Actuality, Possibility, Destiny (or Freedom from Destiny). On the contrary, the succession of Predicates of Predicates is different in the different Modes of Being." (Peirce, *CP* 4.549, "Prolegomena to an Apology for Pragmaticism") [emphasis added]

Penrose, Roger   mathematical physicist, cosmologist; devised Penrose tiling and twistor theory

peregrine   fastest moving creature on earth; the female (larger and more powerful) was a favored bird of falconers in the Middle Ages—only she is given the title of 'falcon'; a male is a tiercel

Persephone   Ionic name in epic literature; in other dialects known under other names, or simply as Kore, girl, when worshipped in the context of Demeter and Kore, mother and daughter; name dangerous to say

Planck, Max   founder of quantum theory

Potter, Beatrix   illustrator, botanist; wrote *The Tale of Peter Rabbit*

Prigogine, Ilya   Nobel prize chemist; studied dissipative structures, self-organizing systems

Prometheus   the other twin Titan brother, the one who could think ahead; see **Epimetheus**

Quipucamayoc   Quipu Keeper, memory expert of the Inkan empire, an accountant who also recounts

RCA   Radio Corporation of America, electronics company, 1919–1986; in 1929, purchased the Victor Talking Machine Company, largest manufacturer of phonographs and phonograph records, thereby acquiring rights to the Nipper trademark, a painting of a dog looking into an Edison Bell cylinder phonograph and, presumably, recognizing 'his master's voice'

Riemann, Georg Friedrich Bernhard   19th c. German mathematician; his theory of higher dimensions (and tensor concept) revolutionized geometry and was used for Einstein's general relativity theory

Rogers, Fred   Presbyterian minister who developed and was host of the *Mister Rogers' Neighborhood* television series for children

Ruth   Bible book; mercy; my mother's name, but not what she was called

Samson   Bible Book of Judges 13–16

Schrödinger, Erwin   Austrian physicist, a founder of quantum mechanics, Nobelist for Schrödinger equation describing how the quantum state of a physical system changes in time

Simone   is **Simone Weil**   philosopher, social activist, mystic; see also *The Red Virgin: A Poem of Simone Weil*

Sondheim, Alan   writer long involved with networked online communication in first and Second Life

Taimina, Daina   Latvian mathematician at Cornell who crochets objects to illustrate hyperbolic space; wrote *Crocheting Adventures with Hyperbolic Planes*. In 1901 Hilbert proved there is no formula to describe the hyperbolic plane (therefore computers cannot model it); yet Taimina can crochet it by adding extra stitches every few rows, causing her material to fold in ways that resemble lettuce leaves, kelp, and coral reefs. Taimina: "I chose to study maths because I thought it was the least political subject. I would never have imagined that something that was purely mathematical would touch on so many other issues." Bellos, "How Crochet Solved an Age-Old Maths Problem," http://accessnewsservice.blogspot.com/2011/02/how-crochet-solved-age-old-maths.html

Talan   is **Talan Memmott**   prolific multimedia digital artist and theorist

Thom, René   Fields Medal mathematician, topologist, founder of catastrophe theory; wrote *Structural Stability and Morphogenesis*

Tiamat   female Water Spirit of primordial chaos; the sea, personified; a monster of Air; Alexander Heidel in *Babylonian Genesis* questions the popular view of Tiamat as a dragon

Tiffany, Louis Comfort   worked in the decorative arts, best known for his work in stained glass

Turing, Alan   mathematician, computer scientist, proponent of machine intelligence; Turing tests are meant to (fail to) discriminate humans from machines

Turrell, James   a James Turrell skyspace is an enclosed room large enough for roughly 15 people—the viewers sit on benches along the edge to view the sky through an opening in the roof; also known for light tunnels

Tzimtzum   Kabbalistic term meaning both withdrawal / contraction and concealment / hiddenness

U   the requisite turn

Vrta   "Without the Asat or its equivalent Vrta, the Dragon, there would be no Indra, nor even the gods for she is their container . . . ," Ernest McClain, *The Myth of Invariance*; " . . . asat: to lose all forms—verbal, audial, or visual—and break the dragon Vrta open again. And *that exercise*, in the *Rig Veda*, is the true meaning of *sacrifice* . . . ,"Antonio T. de Nicolás, *Philosophy East and West*, v.49, n.2, 1999; *Rig Veda*, book of hymns or poems redacted in the Iron Age, 9ᵗʰ to 7ᵗʰ c. BCE, and preserved uncorrupted by two major schools for more than a millennium by oral tradition alone, the two recensions being practically identical

Weyl, Hermann   mathematician-philosopher who studied space, time, and matter; he introduced the notion of gauge in an attempt to model electromagnetic and gravitational fields as geometrical properties of spacetime

Xin Wei   is **Sha Xin Wei**   multimodal artist and mathematician

Yang, Chen Nin "Frank"   Chinese-American Nobelist in physics who showed that elementary particle processes are not left-right symmetric

Z   the z-axis represents getting up off a 2-dimensional plane or down onto a complex one; a z-plane is a conventional representation of complex numbers established by one real axis and an imaginary (z) axis perpendicular to it

Afterword

Unsolved Problems

chance has no memory
so we choose
sealed by amnesia
to undergo the formality of occurring

mysteries bear
in mind have no relation—thus
any linkage—whatsoever
to unsolved problems

in a world divided
into what *can* be divided
without
damage (magnitudes metrics . . .)

what cannot?
what if divided changes its nature?
duration distance solitude
life-

time *obedience* : not ten-hut
military
rather *ob-au-di-re* (hear . . . thoroughly)
then too   endurance

STEPHANIE STRICKLAND is the author of six books of print poetry, most recently *Zone : Zero*, and seven electronic poems, most recently *Sea and Spar Between*, a poetry generator written with Nick Montfort using the words of Emily Dickinson and *Moby-Dick*. Her award-winning works include *V: WaveSon.nets / Losing L'una*—soon to re-appear with a new mobile app—*True North, The Red Virgin: A Poem of Simone Weil,* and "The Ballad of Sand and Harry Soot."

A member of the Board of Directors of the Electronic Literature Organization, Strickland co-edited *Electronic Literature Collection/1*. Two of her collaborative digital pieces appear online in *Electronic Literature Collection/2* (2011), and two others were featured in the Electronic Literature Gallery at MLA in 2012 and 2013. She has written about the new kinds of reading and writing computation makes possible in her essay "Born Digital" on the Poetry Foundation website. She lives in New York City.

AHSAHTA PRESS

SAWTOOTH POETRY PRIZE SERIES

2002: Aaron McCollough, *Welkin* (Brenda Hillman, judge)

2003: Graham Foust, *Leave the Room to Itself* (Joe Wenderoth, judge)

2004: Noah Eli Gordon, *The Area of Sound Called the Subtone* (Claudia Rankine, judge)

2005: Karla Kelsey, *Knowledge, Forms, The Aviary* (Carolyn Forché, judge)

2006: Paige Ackerson-Kiely, *In No One's Land* (D. A. Powell, judge)

2007: Rusty Morrison, *the true keeps calm biding its story* (Peter Gizzi, judge)

2008: Barbara Maloutas, *the whole Marie* (C. D. Wright, judge)

2009: Julie Carr, *100 Notes on Violence* (Rae Armantrout, judge)

2010: James Meetze, *Dayglo* (Terrance Hayes, judge)

2011: Karen Rigby, *Chinoiserie* (Paul Hoover, judge)

2012: T. Zachary Cotler, *Sonnets to the Humans* (Heather McHugh, judge)

AHSAHTA PRESS

NEW SERIES

This book is set in Apollo MT type
with Garamond Premier Pro titles
by Ahsahta Press at Boise State University.
Cover design by Quemadura.
Book design by Janet Holmes.
Printed in Canada.

AHSAHTA PRESS

2013

JANET HOLMES, DIRECTOR
ZACH VESPER, ASSISTANT DIRECTOR

JERRI BENSON, *intern*   STEPHA PETERS
CHRISTOPHER CARUSO   INDRANI SENGUPTA
ZEKE HUDSON   ELIZABETH SMITH
ANNIE KNOWLES   MICHAEL WANZENRIED